AF270511

THE OLYMPIC PARK BOMBING

BY REBECCA MORRIS

AMERICAN CRIME STORIES

Essential Library

An Imprint of Abdo Publishing | abdobooks.com

ABDOBOOKS.COM

Published by Abdo Publishing, a division of ABDO, PO Box 398166, Minneapolis, Minnesota 55439. Copyright © 2024 by Abdo Consulting Group, Inc. International copyrights reserved in all countries. No part of this book may be reproduced in any form without written permission from the publisher. Essential Library™ is a trademark and logo of Abdo Publishing.

Printed in the United States of America, North Mankato, Minnesota.
102023
012024

Cover Photos: Erik S. Lesser/Getty Images News/Getty Images (foreground); Wally McNamee/Corbis Sport/Getty Images (background)
Interior Photos: Barry Chin/Boston Globe/Getty Images, 5; DPA/AFP/Getty Images, 10; Dimitri Iundt/Corbis Sport/VCG/Getty Images, 12, 25; William Berry/Atlanta Journal-Constitution/AP Images, 15; John Bazemore/AP Images, 17; Doug Collier/AFP/Getty Images, 21; Steven R. Schaefer/AFP/Getty Images, 29; FBI, 32; Ric Feld/FBI/AP Images, 35; Brian Schoenhals/Getty Images News/Getty Images, 38; Caroline Baird/AP Images, 41; FBI/Hulton Archive/Getty Images, 45; Arlene Waller/Shutterstock Images, 47; Aaron Bass/Shutterstock Images, 48; Jerry Whaley/Shutterstock Images, 50; Bumble Dee/Shutterstock Images, 53; Alan Marler/AP Images, 57, 61; FBI/Getty Images News/Getty Images, 64; Red Line Editorial, 67; Shutterstock Images, 69; William Silver/Shutterstock Images, 71; John Amis/AP Images, 79; Erik S. Lesser/Getty Images News/Getty Images, 81, 86–87, 89; Barry Williams/Getty Images News/Getty Images, 93; Chuck Burton/AP Images, 94

Editor: Arnold Ringstad
Series Designer: Melissa Martin

Library of Congress Control Number: 2023939444

PUBLISHER'S CATALOGING-IN-PUBLICATION DATA

Names: Morris, Rebecca, author.
Title: The Olympic Park bombing / by Rebecca Morris
Description: Minneapolis, Minnesota: Abdo Publishing, 2024 | Series: American crime stories | Includes online resources and index.
Identifiers: ISBN 9781098292140 (lib. bdg.) | ISBN 9798384910084 (ebook)
Subjects: LCSH: Crime and criminals--Juvenile literature. | Killing (Murder)--Juvenile literature. | United States--Juvenile literature. | Centennial Olympic Park Bombing, Atlanta, Ga., 1996--Juvenile literature. | Terrorist bombings--Juvenile literature. | Serial murderers--Juvenile literature.
Classification: DDC 364.97--dc23

CONTENTS

This book discusses accounts of crime, violence, and death that may be disturbing to some readers.

AN EXPLOSION IN THE NIGHT

Alice Hawthorne and her daughter drove three hours to get to Centennial Olympic Park in Atlanta, Georgia. They lived in the much smaller city of Albany, Georgia, where Alice owned a hot dog and ice cream shop named Fallon's in honor of her daughter. Alice also worked as a customer service representative for a cable company. In her spare time, she liked to volunteer in the community, visiting hospitals, organizing pageants, and supporting historically Black colleges and universities. The trip came as part of an extended birthday celebration for Fallon, who was a big basketball fan. She had turned 14 just three days before.

On the night of July 26, 1996, Alice and Fallon joined 50,000 other people gathered in Centennial Park to celebrate the Olympic Games.[1] The large park, spanning 21 acres (8.5 ha),

Centennial Olympic Park in downtown Atlanta was at the heart of the Olympic Games festivities in 1996.

SUPER STORE

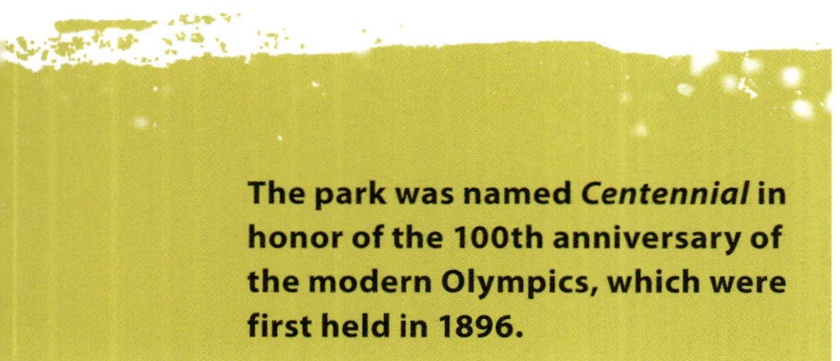

was an exciting place to be.[2] Fans could meet Olympic athletes and get autographs. They could splash in water fountains designed to look like the five iconic rings of the Olympic Games logo. They could admire national flags from all over the world and overhear conversations in a wide variety of languages. Food and drinks were available for purchase in the park.

Every day, the park hosted live concerts. Jack Mack and the Heart Attack, an R&B band, played a concert the night of July 26. Their set continued into the early morning hours of July 27. Alice and Fallon stood by the main stage, enjoying the festivities and taking photos to remember the occasion.

A Suspicious Backpack

Michael Cox was also at the park that night. Cox was sitting with friends on a bench near the concert stage when he noticed a man in his late twenties with an unusual backpack. It was large and boxy with a military green color and style. Cox thought, "Why in the world would somebody be wearing a backpack like that?"[3]

After Cox and his friends left, the man stowed it under the very bench where they had been sitting. Then a new group of young men arrived at the bench. It was a noisy and disruptive group. They drank beer and tossed the cans around. A security guard asked them to leave. As they went, they noticed the backpack beneath their seats. One of the young men tried to take it, but it was so heavy he left it behind.

With the young men leaving, the security guard, whose name was Richard Jewell, saw the backpack. Jewell and Tom Davis, a law enforcement agent who had arrived to help, asked around to see if it belonged to anyone nearby. When no one claimed the backpack, Jewell and Davis initiated the protocol for a suspicious package. That meant calling in bomb experts.

When the young man tried to lift the heavy backpack, he slightly shifted its position. This shift made the explosion less deadly because it changed the direction of a metal plate meant to aim nails at bystanders.

Experts arrived from the Federal Bureau of Investigation (FBI) and the Bureau of Alcohol, Tobacco, and Firearms (ATF). At about 1:00 a.m., one of the agents got on the ground to check carefully inside the backpack without moving it from under the bench. Jewell said the agent "froze" when he saw what was inside and then backed away cautiously.[4] The backpack contained a 40-pound (18 kg) homemade bomb.[5] It was a type of explosive called a pipe bomb, made up of explosive material

packed into hollow tubes. There was an alarm clock rigged
to set off the bomb at a particular time. An engine meant for
model rockets connected to a battery to initiate the blast.

Two Phone Calls

About 15 minutes earlier, a caller had dialed 911 from a pay
phone near the park's north end. The caller had begun to
deliver a message that started, "This is a statement from
the Free Militia, we defy your new world order and you. . ."[6]
However, the call ended before the complete message could
be delivered.

At 12:58 a.m., the same caller dialed 911 again. The second
call came from a different booth but still within just blocks of
the park. This time, the caller gave a warning. He said, "There
is a bomb in Centennial Park. You have 30 minutes."[7] The caller

did not identify himself during this call or the previous one, but he spoke calmly. The voice sounded like that of an American man with no regional accent.

To relay a phone call to responders, the 911 operator needed a street address. However, the operator had trouble locating one. The problem had to do with who controlled the Centennial Park property. The operator's computer had addresses only for property controlled by the city of Atlanta, but the park was under state control rather than city control. After several phone calls, the operator located the address. The delay meant authorities at the park would not get the warning before the explosion.

A Hurried Evacuation

Even though authorities at the park did not yet have the information from the 911 call, other officers had come to help Davis and Jewell. They began clearing the area around the backpack. Initially, Davis and Jewell had moved people away from a 15-foot (4.6 m) space so the bomb experts could do their work.[8] Now officers rushed to push hundreds of people farther back.

Meanwhile, Jewell entered a nearby media tower where crews were working to operate sound and lights for the concert. He evacuated 11 people from the tower.[9] When some of them stopped to turn off equipment or gather belongings,

Jewell urged them to leave the items behind and pushed them along to safety.

Outside the tower, time grew short. With some people refusing to move from their nearby benches, officers used their own bodies to form a barrier between the backpack and the crowd. Around 1:20 a.m., the bomb exploded.

A Deadly Blast

Alice Hawthorne and Fallon were preparing to leave the concert as 1:20 a.m. approached. On their way out, they stopped for a photo. Alice posed by a statue while Fallon reached for her

First responders quickly arrived at Centennial Olympic Park to treat those injured by the blast.

disposable camera. Then the blast went off, and shrapnel struck their bodies. Fallon tried to run but made it only a few steps. Alice had also fallen to the ground. She had grave head wounds. The bomber had placed nails into the pipes to make the blast more deadly. One had pierced the side of Alice's head at her temple.

People rushed to Alice's side to help, but the injuries were too severe. She died at the scene at the age of 44. Before an ambulance rushed Fallon away, she saw her mother dying on the ground. At the hospital, Fallon had surgery to extract shrapnel from her body. She survived the attack.

More than 100 other people were injured.[10] Injuries ranged from shallow shrapnel cuts to broken bones to serious neck, abdominal, and chest wounds. Several people would carry signs and symptoms of their injuries for the rest of their lives. Among the injured were more than 20 police officers who had placed themselves between the crowd and the bomb.[11] Jewell and

A SECOND DEATH

Melih Uzunyol, a 40-year-old camera operator from Turkey, also died the day of the Centennial Park bombing. He had a heart attack while rushing to provide news coverage of the explosion. Officials considered his death to be a homicide. A homicide means another person has caused the death. Investigators reported that the bombing prompted the heart attack and therefore the bomber was responsible. Uzunyol was a husband and a father of two children.

The bomb heavily damaged the media tower that Jewell had evacuated just minutes earlier.

Davis, the two men who began investigating the backpack, both felt the force of the blast, but neither was seriously hurt.

Fears of a New Domestic Terrorist

There had been other bombings in recent years. On April 19, 1995, a bomb exploded at a federal government office building in Oklahoma City, Oklahoma. The explosion partially collapsed the building and killed 168 people, including 19 children.[12] A year later, on April 3, 1996, law enforcement captured a criminal known as the Unabomber, who was responsible for a different type of attack. Over a period of 17 years, the Unabomber killed three people and injured 23 more with homemade bombs he sent through the mail or delivered by hand.[13]

The Oklahoma City bomber, Timothy McVeigh, and the Unabomber, Ted Kaczynski, were both domestic terrorists. A terrorist commits acts of violence to promote political, racial, or religious views. Domestic terrorists commit these acts against citizens or institutions in their native countries. McVeigh was motivated by political extremism and distrust of the US government. Kaczynski targeted scientists and technology researchers and also disliked government officials and law enforcement.

McVeigh's attack had been one of the deadliest single acts of domestic terrorism in US history. The manhunt to capture Kaczynski was among the FBI's longest and most expensive ever. With the bombing at Centennial Olympic Park, officials suspected another domestic terrorist was responsible.

CONTINUING THE GAMES

Government officials decided the Olympic Games would continue after the bombing. President Bill Clinton said, "The games will go on. The Olympic spirit will prevail. We must be firm in this; we cannot be intimidated by acts of terror."[14] Decades earlier in Munich, Germany, officials of the 1972 Olympic Games made a similar decision. During those games, a Palestinian terrorist group held members of the Israeli Olympic team hostage. Twelve people were killed, including athletes, referees, coaches, and a police officer.[15] The Olympics paused for a day to honor the victims and then continued.

CHAPTER TWO

THE ACCUSATION

nvestigators began work immediately after the explosion. Their first steps involved securing the crime scene and collecting evidence. They gathered shrapnel and debris from the bomb, including nails, screws, pipes, duct tape, wires, and a timer. They also took statements from victims and witnesses in the park, and they investigated the bomber's 911 calls.

After a crime, it is also standard procedure for investigators to interview responders. Jewell had four interviews with investigators in the hours after the bombing.[1] Jewell took the agents through his experience of the night's events. He told them how he asked the noisy group of young men to leave, saw the backpack, showed it to Davis, and watched the bomb experts investigate it. He also explained his role in helping

Security guard Richard Jewell soon found himself in the spotlight as investigators searched for the bomber.

clear the area around the backpack and evacuate the media
tower nearby.

Media Attention

That same day, officials appeared on television to provide
information to the public and the media. During a press
conference on Saturday afternoon, Davis noted that a security
guard had spotted the suspicious backpack. That same
day, President Bill Clinton issued remarks on the bombing.
As he spoke, he acknowledged the security guard's role in
saving lives.

Neither Davis nor the president had used Jewell's name,
but the media tracked down his identity. The Olympics were
a major international event, and journalists from around the
world had gathered in Atlanta to cover the competition. Now
coverage turned to the bombing. The first request for an
interview with Jewell came from CNN, a national news outlet
that was based in Atlanta. They asked Jewell to appear live on
their broadcast at 8:00 p.m. Saturday night. Not even a full day
had passed since the 1:20 a.m. bombing.

Following the interview, many other media outlets
contacted Jewell and asked to speak with him too. They
praised him for his actions in spotting the backpack and
getting people to safety. The newspaper *USA Today* reported,
"The biggest hero of the Atlanta Olympics is a man of modest

height and stocky build, with no sport other than occasional pickup basketball. He will get no medal and stand on no award platform."[2]

Suspicion

Shortly after Jewell's first CNN interview, the FBI received a phone call from Jewell's former employer, Piedmont College.

As suspicion around Jewell began to grow, the news media started closely following him.

The college's president, Ray Cleere, had watched the interview on television. Cleere believed he had important information about Jewell's background that investigators might need to know.

Jewell, who was 33 years old, had worked for Piedmont College as a campus officer. The job had not gone smoothly, and his employment there ended in May 1996 after less than a year. The college repeatedly warned Jewell about overstepping his authority. As a campus officer, Jewell was authorized to work only inside the college campus, but he ignored those boundaries many times. He would stop drivers on nearby city streets and give them citations for traffic violations. These streets were not part of the campus. Only local police had the authority to make those traffic stops. Jewell further interfered with local police work by listening to their radio communications and attempting to help when they responded to situations.

Other sources also cast Jewell and his work record in a negative light. The Piedmont College police chief, Jewell's supervisor at the college, reported that Jewell had knowledge of bomb making. A manager connected to Jewell's work at Centennial Olympic Park told the FBI that Jewell was very intense and possessive of the park area he monitored. The manager also thought Jewell might have had something to do with the explosion.

Following this information, the FBI learned more about Jewell and his work background. The background check showed that Jewell was dedicated to a policing career, but it also showed problems. Before his job with Piedmont College, Jewell worked for the Habersham County Sheriff's Office in a small rural part of northeastern Georgia. He worked there for more than five years, moving his way up from jailer to road deputy. Whenever he got the opportunity, he took classes and earned extra credentials. To fellow officers, though, Jewell sometimes seemed reckless. He had to resign from his road deputy job after one of multiple accidents in his patrol car.

According to interviews with former coworkers and acquaintances, Jewell seemed obsessive about policing. A past roommate reported that Jewell spent too much time analyzing recorded episodes of the reality television show *Cops*. Jewell once had been jailed overnight for impersonating an officer when he made an arrest before receiving his official authority to do so.

He enjoyed the rush of responding to calls. In a conversation with a friend, he had said he would want to be in the middle of the action if there were an emergency at the Olympics. Cleere said that Jewell "always wanted to be a hero."[4] Investigators believed these were all signs of a man who might plant a bomb to gain attention.

Profiling Jewell

Even before the FBI received these tips on Jewell, it had agents from the Behavioral Science Unit (BSU) on the case. Their job was to consider the psychological profile of the criminal. A psychological profile gives insight into a criminal's mind and motivations. BSU agents considered what kind of person would commit this type of attack and why.

Once the agents received information about Jewell, they focused on one particular profile. The profile is called hero homicide or the hero complex. This profile describes someone who creates a false emergency so they can lead the rescue and become a hero. It is not uncommon for the

A Georgia Tech professor used a computer program to estimate the 911 caller's height based on how deep the voice was. The program estimated the height as about six feet, one inch (1.85 m).

person to have a background in law enforcement or security. In Jewell's case, some began to call it the hero-bomber profile.

Public Accusations

The media quickly learned of suspicion around Jewell. On Tuesday, July 30, the *Atlanta Journal-Constitution* published an article titled "FBI Suspects 'Hero' Guard May Have Planted Bomb."[5] That evening, a CNN anchor displayed the paper on camera for viewers to see. Within the span of three days, news presentations of Jewell went from heroic to criminal.

Jewell knew investigators had to question him because he had been in the area of the bombing. He knew it was standard procedure to rule out the people close to a crime. He had

A lawyer for Jewell held up the *Atlanta Journal-Constitution* headline at a press conference and vowed to sue the newspaper.

learned this procedure in his police training. However, Jewell did not get any forewarning about the level of suspicion before the news stories began.

As word of the *Atlanta Journal-Constitution*'s article spread, reporters, photographers, and television crews found the apartment where Jewell lived with his mother. They gathered outside and stayed day and night. They followed Jewell if he tried to go anywhere. The FBI also assigned agents to observe and follow him. They obtained warrants to search his apartment and storage unit for evidence of bomb-making materials. They took hair samples and had Jewell repeat the transcript of the 911 call to see if his voice matched the caller's.

Clearing Jewell

The attention on Jewell continued for 88 days.[6] In that time, investigators never uncovered evidence to charge him with a crime. They concluded that Jewell could not have made the 911 calls because he was with law enforcement at the park at that time. There was no evidence he had used an accomplice in the calls. The searches of his apartment and storage unit revealed no evidence that he had constructed the bomb.

On October 26, three months after the Olympic Park bombing, the authorities released a statement saying that Jewell was no longer a target of the investigation. The statement said, "In this case, the Jewells [Richard and his mother] have regrettably also endured highly unusual and intense publicity."[7] During the ordeal, Jewell's attorney said, "I just hope that while the FBI puts a thousand people on Richard Jewell that the real guy doesn't get away or is planning some other act."[8]

CHAPTER THREE

TWO MORE ATTACKS IN ATLANTA

By the start of the new year, investigators still had not made an arrest in the Olympic Park bombing. On December 9, 1996, the FBI released the audio recordings of the 911 phone calls in the hope that they might bring new leads. The bureau thought someone in the general public might recognize the voice. It also offered a $500,000 reward for information that would help it make an arrest.[1] Thousands of tips came in, but none produced a suspect. Then came more attacks.

The Clinic Attack

The workday was just beginning at Sandy Springs Professional Building on a cold Thursday morning, January 16, 1997. This three-story building, located in the Sandy Springs suburb north of Atlanta, had law and medical offices inside. One of the

A careful examination of the Olympic Park scene by multiple law enforcement agencies turned up no useful leads.

medical offices was Northside Family Planning Services, a clinic that provided reproductive health services, including abortions. The clinic was on the first floor.

Just before 9:30 a.m., the building trembled. Windows broke, and portions of the ceilings and walls collapsed. A bomb had exploded at Northside Family Planning Services. People ran frightened and screaming from the building out into the cold. Remarkably, no one was hurt.

Firefighters, local police, and federal law enforcement responded to the scene. Media also arrived to report on the incident. As responders worked to secure the area, a second bomb exploded, this time in the parking lot. It was a stronger blast than the first.

Several emergency responders and a news camera operator were injured in the second explosion. One of the injured people, an FBI agent, suffered head wounds from the nails used to make the bomb and had permanent hearing loss. Officials called the attack a double bombing because two devices had been set to explode. They determined the second bomb was placed to target law enforcement.

The investigation later revealed that the bomber had staked out the office building for more than a week beforehand. The bomber wore wigs and changed clothing to disguise his identity. During this time, the bomber had observed a previous fire alarm. He watched to see how first responders would approach the building during an emergency situation. From his observations, he knew that law enforcement would be on the scene of his first bombing within an hour. The bomber set the timer in the second device to target those responders.

The Nightclub Attack

Just over a month later, on February 21, 1997, yet another bombing attack occurred, this time in midtown Atlanta. It was a Friday night, and more than 100 people were inside the Otherside Lounge, a gay and lesbian nightclub.[2] Some people were enjoying live piano music in one room while others were dancing under a disco ball in another room.

Clubgoers did not notice a green backpack in the bushes by the parking lot at the front of the club. An unknown man had placed it there secretly earlier in the day. That night, the same man returned and left a package by the patio in the back of the club. Clubgoers had not seen him this second time either.

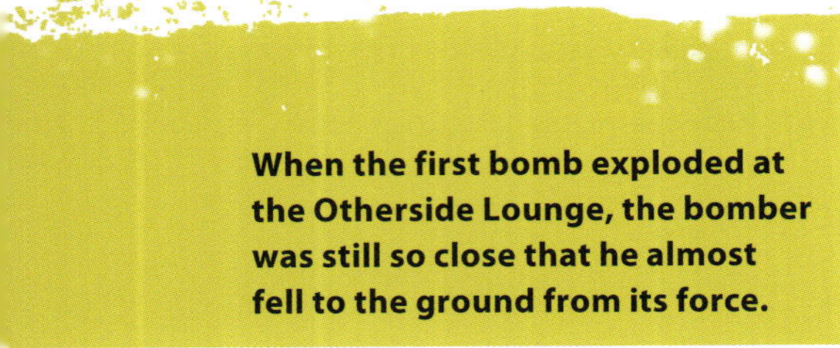

Around 10:00 p.m., a loud noise came from the patio. Clubgoers likened the noise to a gunshot or a cannon blast. Nails exploded from the bomb and into the club. One lodged in a woman's arm. Other projectiles flew farther into the parking lot outside. The nightclub's owner had just arrived and parked her own car when the explosion occurred. She witnessed the violent force of the explosion and falling debris damage her car and a number of other vehicles. Inside the club, five people were injured.[3]

Law enforcement responded to the emergency and discovered a second, unexploded bomb in the front parking lot. It was inside the green backpack hidden in the bushes. Responders believed it was placed there to target them, similar to the second bomb at the Sandy Springs clinic. A render safe team, which is a special group of law enforcement experts, arrived to handle the unexploded bomb. They used a remote-controlled robot and a water cannon to explode the second bomb safely without hurting anyone else.

Letters from the Bomber

Three days later, on February 24, the FBI received several copies of a handwritten letter from the bomber. The bomber had used

The FBI held a press conference to demonstrate the similarities between the bombs that had been used in the three attacks.

a thick felt-tipped pen and lined paper. He wrote in choppy block letters. Originally, the bomber sent the letter to four news agencies: Reuters, NBC News, the *Atlanta Journal-Constitution*, and a local CBS channel. These agencies forwarded the letters to the FBI. Each letter was postmarked February 23 from Atlanta.

The bomber had not signed his name to the letters, but he included the name of a group, the Army of God. The Army of God began in the early 1980s as a movement of Christian extremism. Its members believed violence was justified to combat government policies they viewed as anti-Christian. The letters said that units of this group had perpetrated the January and February bombings in Atlanta.

The letters also identified a motive for the bombings. The bombs were retaliation against the federal government for policies allowing abortion and same-sex relationships. The bomber purposefully chose an abortion facility and a business catering to gay and lesbian people. The letters said that the second bombs at each location targeted federal law enforcement officers who responded to the first explosions. The letters contained warnings that bombings would continue.

In addition, the letters gave details of the bombs' construction. The writer listed specific information about the dynamite, containers, batteries, timers, and nails. Law enforcement had not released those specifics publicly. The bomber, however, would have that information. Because of these details, the FBI determined that the letters were authentic messages from the bomber.

The FBI examined the letters for evidence that could identify the bomber. Agents checked for fingerprints but did not find any from the bomber. The only prints were those of workers who had touched the envelopes. Investigators reached a dead end with the address too. The return address on the letters, 170 Eighth Street, Atlanta, GA, was made up. The postal station that had sorted the letters, North Metro station, was so large that there was no way to track the letters' origin through that facility. Even with the letters, investigators still did not have enough evidence to identify the bomber.

A Coincidence, a Copycat, or a Serial Bomber

The letter took credit for the January and February bombings, but it did not claim responsibility for the attack at Centennial Olympic Park. It did not even mention the Olympic Park bombing at all. However, law enforcement investigated potential connections between the attacks because of similarities between them.

One similarity was the use of nails. A spokesperson for the ATF said, "I know it's obvious to everyone, so I will go ahead and confirm it: there were nails in some of the bombs in all three incidents."[5] There were also steel plates in bombs at each site. The plates were meant to make the bombs more destructive. They aimed the nails in one direction to concentrate the force. Bombs at all three attack sites also contained the same brand of alarm clock to serve as a timer triggering the detonation.

One difference between the Olympic Park bombing in July 1996 and the two later bombings was the placement of a second bomb. Both the January and February 1997 bombings

The FBI took the pay phone used to make the 911 calls at Centennial Olympic Park as evidence in the case.

TOOLMARK ANALYSIS

Toolmark forensic examiners study objects from crime scenes. They look for markings that may give information about the tools used to make an object or a suspect who has handled it. While working on the Atlanta bombing case, examiner John Collins developed a process to detect microscopic markings on nails. These markings form as the nails are cut and shaped during manufacturing. The markings are unique to the manufacturer that produces the nail. If investigators were able to find a suspect with nails matching those from a bomb site, they could use that finding as evidence. In the bombing investigations, nails became crucial evidence and one of the first forensic links to the bomber.

had involved second devices positioned to attack first responders. There had been no second bomb at Centennial Olympic Park. However, investigators believed the bomber may have placed the 911 calls before the bombing to concentrate responders at the scene and put them in danger.

By this time, more than 50 federal agents were working on the investigation.[6] The agents were still considering all possibilities. The similarities in the bombs might be a coincidence. They could be the work of a copycat bomber. A copycat is a criminal who replicates the behavior of another criminal. Finally, there was the possibility of a serial bomber, one person who had carried out all three attacks in the Atlanta area. It was possible that person could be evolving their technique, which would account for the differences. If it was a serial bomber, investigators worried the attacks might continue.

THE PURSUIT BEGINS

Months passed without further attacks. The one-year anniversary of the Olympic Park bombing came and went. To mark the anniversary, Atlanta mayor Bill Campbell held a memorial service in the park. Alice Hawthorne's husband, John, spoke at the service, and her daughter Fallon also attended.

Investigators had identified no new suspects since Jewell had been cleared. But they continued to pursue leads and release information to the public in the hope that it might bring fresh evidence. Among the information was a new sketch of a man observed at the Olympic Park bombing. The man was white and in his twenties. An older version of the sketch showed the man with a goatee. The newer version released around the one-year anniversary of the bombing showed

In June 1997, the authorities released a new sketch of the man seen at the Sandy Springs Professional Building.

the man without a goatee. Investigators offered a reward of $100,000 for information leading to an arrest.[1]

They also continued to issue warnings to law enforcement throughout the country. The warnings instructed law enforcement to watch for the pattern established in the Atlanta-area bombings. Specifically, the warnings said to be cautious about potential second explosions.

Starting the Workday

Robert Sanderson got his morning coffee and arrived to work as a security guard at the New Woman All Women Health Clinic shortly after 7:00 a.m. on January 29, 1998. The Birmingham, Alabama, clinic needed security guards because it provided abortions. The clinic often had people protesting against abortion outside its office. The security guards were there to make sure that protests remained peaceful.

Sanderson, who was in his mid-thirties, took the security guard position as a second job to earn extra income. His primary job was serving as an officer with the Birmingham Police Department. He lived with his wife and two stepsons. He went by the nickname "Sande" and was well liked in the community. In fact, he had received a special honor because of his reputation for service. In 1996, officials had picked him as a representative to carry the Olympic Torch when it passed through Birmingham on its route to the Atlanta Games.

Emily Lyons arrived at the clinic shortly after Sanderson.
Lyons was a 41-year-old nurse, wife, and mother known for
her sense of humor. It was her job to open the clinic that day. As she walked to the building just after 7:30 a.m., she saw something unusual on the ground. It was a mound of fake leaves. Lyons alerted Sanderson to the unusual sight.

Lyons remained about 10 feet (3 m) away as Sanderson approached to investigate. When Sanderson bent in to see the object, a bomb exploded. The explosion forced Sanderson's body 15 feet (4.6 m) through the air.[2] Sanderson was badly burned, and his injuries were catastrophic. He died at the scene. A newspaper later apologized for publishing a photograph of his body because the scene was so gruesome.

Lyons was also burned and had dozens of wounds to her legs, abdomen, and face. She was bleeding heavily, but she

Lyons underwent more than 30 hours of surgeries in the six months following the attack.

was alive. Bystanders hurried to provide aid while they waited for first responders. One of these bystanders observed a man with long hair and a backpack walking away from the clinic.

The Bomber Escapes

The bomber had watched the entire scene. He saw Sanderson on duty in front of the clinic. He saw Lyons arrive to open the clinic for the day. It was a familiar scene to the bomber. He had observed the clinic's opening procedure a month beforehand in preparation for the attack. The bomber used the observations to determine where to place the bomb. He selected a location by the entrance. Then he put the explosive in a toolbox and used artificial leaves to disguise it.

US attorney general Janet Reno called investigators at the clinic bombing site. Reno was communicating directly with President Clinton about the bombing in real time.

On the morning of January 29, the bomber saw Lyons observe the suspicious mound of leaves and alert Sanderson. He watched Sanderson bend over to inspect the area. That is when he used a remote control to trigger the explosion. The bomber was close enough that the explosion knocked him to the ground. He stood and left the scene.

Trailing the Bomber

Like the bystander who had rushed to help victims, 18-year-old Jermaine Hughes had also noticed a man walking away from the clinic. At the time of the explosion, Hughes was more than a block away in a college dormitory washing his clothes. He was

There was no second device at the Birmingham clinic as there had been at the Sandy Springs clinic and Otherside Lounge. Those earlier devices had timers that needed to be set beforehand to trigger the explosions. The Olympic Park bomb also had a timer. In Birmingham, the device had a remote control. The remote allowed the bomber to trigger the explosion by hand at any given time. Investigators suspected the bomber planned to watch and explode the device when the clinic was full. They believed Sanderson's discovery prompted the bomber to trigger the explosion earlier than planned.

a student at the University of Alabama, Birmingham. Upon hearing the blast, Hughes ran to the window. He saw smoke rising, and then he saw the suspicious man.

The man caught Hughes's attention because his behavior was so different from everyone else's. His movements were calm and methodical. Others were looking toward the clinic or rushing to the scene, but this man was moving away purposefully. The man wore a black baseball cap over long hair. He had on a long coat and held an empty backpack. When the man quickened his pace, Hughes hurried to his car to follow him.

From his car, Hughes observed as the man, who was on foot, turned into an alley. When the man reemerged, Hughes saw that his appearance had been a disguise. The man had removed his coat and hat, and his hair was now short.

The change of appearance added to Hughes's suspicions. When Hughes lost track of him, he drove to a McDonald's to call 911.

Jeff Tickal, a lawyer, was at the McDonald's having breakfast before work. He heard Hughes mention the explosion and the suspicious man. Then, he heard Hughes call out to the 911 operator, "I got him, I got him!"[5] Hughes had just seen the man walk by. Tickal saw him too, but then lost sight of him when the man left the sidewalk and headed into nearby woods.

Authorities searched the bombed Birmingham clinic for clues, but it was witnesses on the ground who provided the vital information to move the case forward.

Tickal got into his car to search for the man. Shortly after, police arrived at the McDonald's and spoke with Hughes. They too went in search of the man, first on foot and then by car. Hughes also got back in his car to look for the man.

Tickal regained sight of the man, who had emerged from a different part of the woods and was now placing items into a gray Nissan truck. Then the man got into the truck and drove away. Tickal drove after the truck and observed the license plate. It was from North Carolina. He wrote the plate number on the coffee cup he had taken from McDonald's.

Hughes was in the area too. He saw Tickal's car behind the man's truck. Hughes pulled up next to the truck to see the driver. He recognized him as the suspicious man. Just as Tickal had done, Hughes made sure to write down the license plate number. Hughes and Tickal both provided law enforcement with the license plate number.

It was valuable information. Through the license plate number, officials identified the truck's owner that same day. The owner's name was Eric Robert Rudolph. According to information from Rudolph's driver's license, he was 31 years old and five feet, 11 inches (1.8 m) tall. He had brown hair and blue eyes. The address connected to the driver's license was in Asheville, a city in western North Carolina.

CHAPTER FIVE

A LONE TERRORIST

Eric Rudolph's family bought land in North Carolina shortly after his father, Bob, died of cancer in 1981. Rudolph was 14 at the time. He was part of a large family with three older brothers, an older sister, and a younger brother. Before moving to North Carolina, the Rudolphs had lived in Florida, where Bob worked for an airline at Miami International Airport. He later got a job at the Miami Zoo doing construction work.

The Rudolphs' North Carolina property was in Topton. Topton is located in Cherokee County, the westernmost county in the state. The area is a remote, forested part of the Blue Ridge Mountains. The Rudolphs were drawn to the region after visiting a former Florida neighbor, Tom Branham, who had moved there. Branham lived a survivalist lifestyle.

Rudolph's upbringing had a significant influence on his eventual crimes.

The lifestyle emphasized self-sufficiency and apocalyptic, anti-government ideas.

Extremist Ideas and a Life off the Grid

Before his family moved, Rudolph would travel to see Branham regularly, even staying for weeks during the summer and when his father was ill. When Bob died, Rudolph lived with Branham until Rudolph's mother, Pat, arrived from Florida. Pat had remained in Florida to take care of family business and to allow Rudolph's sister to complete her last weeks of high school there. Once in North Carolina, Pat purchased land next to Branham's.

From Branham, Rudolph learned about wilderness survival skills, raising animals, construction, auto repair, and farming. Branham did not hold a steady job and instead supported himself through occasional construction work, searching grocery store dumpsters for food, and a variety of other activities. Rudolph admired

BOB RUDOLPH'S DEATH

Some thought Bob Rudolph's death could be the reason for the Rudolph family's anti-government views. Pat and Bob wanted to treat his cancer with laetrile, a controversial cancer drug not approved for use in the United States. Bob went to Mexico to get laetrile. The family may have believed easier access to the drug could have saved Bob's life.

these practices as examples of a liberating, independent, and resourceful way to live. He called it a "pioneer life."[1]

The Rudolphs followed Branham's example. They lived off the grid, which meant they did as much as possible to run their home without outside resources. They made their own home water system that worked without electricity. They had a wood-burning stove to create heat. They grew their own food.

The westernmost region of North Carolina features vast forested areas where people can choose to settle far away from modern life.

Some people who follow the survivalist lifestyle create stockpiles of guns and ammunition to prepare for what they believe will be apocalyptic events.

The family was suspicious of many institutions, including the government and modern medicine.

Branham also held strong political views. He viewed the federal government as "oppressive" and a "tyranny."[2] He had constructed his home from cinderblocks and steel, and he stored supplies in case of an apocalypse. Extremist movements in the area believed this apocalypse would result from a confrontation between the government and citizens.

Branham's supplies included nonperishable food, fuel, and weapons. When Eric was an older teenager, he witnessed ATF agents searching Branham's property. They confiscated guns, dynamite, and instructions for making bombs.

The Rudolphs and their acquaintances also held strong religious views. For example, a local man named George Nordmann, who had children around Rudolph's age, was outspoken about religion. He displayed anti-abortion information in his health food store along with Christian religious items. He made statements denying the events of the Holocaust, the mass murder of Jews during World War II (1939–1945).

Pat shopped at Nordmann's store and had shared some religious background with him. Nordmann was Catholic, and Pat had studied to be a Catholic nun before marrying. Pat then began to explore other branches of Christianity. In Florida, she and Bob had belonged to the same faith community as Branham. The community would hold long meetings at members' homes. During the meetings, members would speak about their personal religious experiences.

Pat later became interested in the Christian Identity movement. She said she was interested in the movement's focus on homeschooling. However, the movement was also racist, homophobic, anti-Semitic, and militant. Its members believed that only white people of European descent were chosen by God. The group justified violence against any activities the movement viewed as ungodly, including abortion. The movement also emphasized storing supplies and weapons to be prepared for an apocalyptic confrontation between good and evil.

School Days

After moving to North Carolina, Rudolph began ninth grade at Nantahala High. The school shared a name with the Nantahala Forest that surrounded the area. Rudolph came to know the

Rudolph spent a lot of time in Nantahala National Forest as a teenager, gaining experience living outdoors.

area well. He had a habit of going off to camp in the woods for entire weekends there without even a change of clothes. He would also share his knowledge about the outdoors and survival skills with schoolmates.

Rudolph showed a different side in his classwork. He conveyed extremist ideas about politics and different groups of people. He used racist, homophobic, and sexist language around classmates and teachers. He gave a report denying that the Holocaust had happened. Rudolph also missed many days of school due to travel. The family made frequent trips to Florida because Rudolph's sister still lived there.

Rudolph left school in tenth grade when his mother began homeschooling him and his younger brother, Jamie. In late 1984, Pat followed advice from Branham and took the two boys to Schell City, Missouri, to continue their homeschooling education within the community of the Church of Israel. The Church of Israel followed the Christian Identity movement.

Rudolph had trouble adhering to the strict rules

Rudolph met and fell in love with a young woman named Joy in Schell City. They even kept in touch when Rudolph moved back to North Carolina, and they became engaged. The relationship did not last, and Joy married someone else. She died by suicide years after that. Investigators who searched Rudolph's belongings after the bombings found one of Joy's sweaters.

of the Church of Israel. The community's leader described him as "undisciplined," "belligerent," and "unable to get along with others at the church."[3] The family returned to North Carolina in the spring of 1985, less than a year after they had left.

A Violent Turn

Rudolph eventually earned his GED and attended two semesters of college at Western Carolina University. In 1987, he left college to join the US Army. He completed basic training in Fort Benning, Georgia, and then received assignment to the 101st Airborne Division in Fort Campbell, Kentucky.

Rudolph and other soldiers trained in survival tactics and weapons. Weapons training included how to make improvised explosive devices (IEDs) using dynamite and everyday items such as nails. He also learned how to create traps by using two explosions. The first explosion was meant to attract enemy attention, and the second would occur once they gathered in response.

In the military, Rudolph continued to express racist, sexist, and anti-Semitic ideas. He also expressed anti-government ideas. He believed the government was too powerful. He disrespected the military's hierarchy and did not like taking orders from Black or female superiors. Officers noted Rudolph's disrespectful attitude toward authority figures. In 1988, Rudolph was discharged because of this attitude and a failed drug test. He had failed the drug test on purpose by smoking marijuana beforehand.

After his discharge, Rudolph moved back to Topton, where he did carpentry work and grew marijuana to sell. Girlfriends and acquaintances who knew Rudolph around this time gave various descriptions of him. They said that sometimes he could be funny and smart. A woman in Topton who hired Rudolph and his brothers to do some construction work on her trailer described the young men as tidy and respectful. She said,

Rudolph's short-lived military experience taught him more about using weapons, including explosives.

"They seemed like somebody who would be honest and do the work right."[4]

At the same time, Rudolph also had a side that could frighten his peers. Sometimes he would go into long speeches filled with angry language against many groups of people and the government. He mentioned an interest in bomb making and the types of nail-filled bombs he would like to construct. He also never could persuade any of his girlfriends to take up the off-the-grid lifestyle he had embraced from his childhood.

Even Branham noticed a change in Rudolph. He thought Rudolph had grown more extreme in his twenties. He was more withdrawn, negative, and suspicious of other people. He could also be violent. Branham reported incidents of Rudolph shooting family pets.

A Secret Life

Rudolph began to hide aspects of his life from his family. In May 1996, he told them he would be traveling west in search of land to buy. He used pay phones to call them with updates claiming that he had made it to Idaho. However, there was never proof he had actually gone there. He seemed to have stayed around the western North Carolina area.

In June, Rudolph used a fake name, Bob Randolph, to rent a trailer in Murphy, North Carolina. It was about 40 miles (64 km) from the home his family had lived in.[5] Rudolph paid in cash, something he always did so that others could not trace him through bank accounts or credit cards. In July, an acquaintance ran into Rudolph when he was leaving the tools and hardware section of the Walmart in Murphy. It was just a week before the Centennial Olympic Park bombing.

From the summer of 1996 to January 1998, the period of time when the Atlanta and Birmingham bombings occurred, Rudolph would drop in on family for holidays or trips and then leave without explanation. Sometimes months would go by between visits. He moved often from rental property to rental property, always paying in cash.

LONE WOLF TERRORISM

Law enforcement distinguishes lone wolf terrorism from organized terrorism. Lone wolf terrorists plan and carry out attacks without instructions or help from others. In some cases, they may have limited assistance from one or two others. Organized terror groups such as Al-Qaeda have leaders who coordinate attacks. Both lone wolf terrorists and organized terrorists convey a political or religious message. That message is what makes terrorism different from other types of crimes.

CHAPTER SIX

LAUNCHING A MANHUNT

n January 1998, there were only a few FBI agents assigned full-time to western North Carolina. One of the agents in that region, Jim Russell, arrived at the address connected to Rudolph's truck. He found that it was an apartment complex where Rudolph's mother, Pat, had once lived. However, it was not the fugitive's current place of residence. The search for Rudolph continued.

Russell began to track down people who knew Rudolph in hopes of finding out where he was. He spoke with Rudolph's brother-in-law and then with a former school acquaintance. The school acquaintance said Rudolph might be living around Murphy, a small town in Cherokee County. The county sheriff in Cherokee, Jack Thompson, located the address for a trailer Rudolph was renting.

After identifying Rudolph, law enforcement agencies put vast amounts of effort and resources into tracking him down.

By this time, Russell had assistance from two other agents. One, Tom Frye, was from the North Carolina State Bureau of Investigation (SBI). The other, John Felton, was an ATF agent stationed in Asheville. The three agents drove to the address Thompson gave them. Frye remained in the car while Russell and Felton approached the trailer. They both had training on entering potentially dangerous buildings. They wore body armor and carried rifles as they moved toward the trailer.

It was January 30, just one day after the Birmingham bombing. Agents found the trailer empty. However, there were signs that Rudolph had been there recently. The lights and heat were on, and the door was open. In the kitchen, there was uncooked oatmeal next to a pot of water. These signs suggested that Rudolph had left recently and quickly. Frye kept watch on the trailer from the woods overnight, but Rudolph did not return.

A Hasty Departure

Right after the bombing in Birmingham, Rudolph had driven more than 200 miles (322 km) back to North Carolina.[1] When he arrived at his trailer, Rudolph thought over what had happened as he left the bombing scene. He wondered how much the witnesses knew. He wondered if they had given law enforcement enough information to identify him. He turned on the radio to listen for news about the bombing and whether law enforcement was looking for a specific person of interest. Rudolph did not hear his name, but he spent the night of January 29 hiding supplies and sleeping in the woods.

The next day Rudolph heard on the radio that authorities were searching for a particular unnamed suspect. He knew he had to move soon. He gathered clothing and cash from his trailer and drove away. Then, while driving, he heard his own name on the radio. Rudolph waited in the woods until night. When it was dark, he went to a store to purchase a large supply of nonperishable food, such as canned tuna, oatmeal, raisins, and nuts. He also got other items he might need, such as batteries. After that, he abandoned his truck and fled into the Nantahala Forest on foot. It was January 30, 1998.

Two local hunters discovered Rudolph's truck deserted in woods near Murphy about a week after he disappeared.

Scouring the Mountains

Meanwhile, law enforcement began coordinating its approach to a large-scale manhunt. It was one of the biggest in national history. Nantahala National Forest is a vast and rugged part of the Appalachian Mountains. The forest spans 531,148 acres (214,948 ha) and is the biggest national forest of the four in North Carolina.[2] Parts of the area are so wild and hard to

Rudolph tried to avoid transactions such as bank accounts that would leave records about him. However, there were records despite his precautions. For example, law enforcement discovered Rudolph rented movies frequently. They examined rental store records to see when he had checked out and returned movies. These records helped them track his activities around the time of the Birmingham bombing. They also found a receipt for groceries Rudolph had purchased before disappearing. Nutrition experts for the FBI calculated the calories in the groceries to estimate how long Rudolph could survive on what he bought. They estimated six months.[3]

navigate that plane crashes have been known to go unrecovered for decades.

Hundreds of law enforcement agents gathered in western North Carolina to conduct the manhunt. Among them were specialized teams. There were helicopter teams that flew over the area. Heat-sensing technology on some of the helicopters was designed to detect heat emitted from the body of a living person. This heat-sensing technology could provide agents with information in areas of dense foliage where it was hard to see. Other search technology included electronic motion sensors and night-vision goggles.

There were also specialized teams that handled dogs trained to track humans. In addition to these teams, agents allowed local hunters and their dogs to enter the search area. Hunters knew the forest and mountains well and could alert officials to signs of Rudolph.

With Rudolph known to be capable of violence, teams who entered the forest to track him were heavily armed.

Law enforcement agents who ventured into the forest on foot had heavy gear. A journalist described them as being "armed to the teeth."[4] They wore military clothes and carried high-powered rifles as they searched the woods for Rudolph.

News media gathered in the area as law enforcement conducted its work. The media presence focused national attention on the large-scale nature of the search. It also

Some local businesses made light of the situation. They sold merchandise with slogans such as "Run, Rudolph, Run" and "1998 Hide and Seek Champion Eric Rudolph."[5]

created some disruption in the small-town communities nearby.
A local police chief described the scene of satellite news trucks
and scores of reporters stationed in his town as a "madhouse."[6]

Searching Rudolph's Property

As agents searched the Nantahala Forest, others focused on
connecting Rudolph to materials used in making the bombs.
They would need this evidence to make a legal case against him
in court if he were found alive. Agents had search warrants for
Rudolph's trailer, storage unit, and truck. In these searches, they
found dynamite residue on several items. They found nails that
seemed to match those used in at least one of the bombings.
After studying the steel plates used to concentrate nails in
the bombs, they discovered the plates had been stocked at a

TENSION WITH THE LOCAL COMMUNITY

The mayor of Murphy, Bill Hughes, criticized media portrayals of the local area. He said,
"They painted a picture of us being illiterate hillbillies down here. . . . They said we were
able to identify with Rudolph and we're sympathetic to him, which was totally false."[7]
The mayor of Andrews, Jim Dailey, also addressed reports that local residents supported
violence against abortion providers. He said, "There's some talk about local people who
thought he might be a folk hero. I don't agree with that." Dailey added that he personally
believed abortions were wrong, "But that don't give him [Rudolph] the right to go out and
kill somebody."[8]

hardware company Rudolph had access to. They learned he had ordered books on how to make homemade bombs.

Law enforcement officials in Atlanta and Birmingham were doing similar work to make legal cases proving Rudolph was the bomber. In March 1998, the Department of Justice created the Southeast Bomb Task Force (SBTF) to coordinate the North Carolina search with state, local, and federal officials. In a press release, the department said the SBTF's purpose was to "pool their resources into one region-wide investigation of a series of Southeastern bombings over the past two years."[9] Law enforcement officials suspected Rudolph was behind all the bombings, but they needed forensic evicence to prove it.

Visit to a Neighbor

Despite the effort, law enforcement was unable to find Rudolph through the spring of 1998. On May 5, 1998, the FBI added Rudolph to its Ten Most Wanted Fugitives list and offered a $1 million reward for information that would help locate him.[10] It was a large reward for information on a Ten Most Wanted fugitive. The typical amount was $50,000.[11] FBI director Louis Freeh and US attorney general Janet Reno announced the large reward amount in a joint press conference.

Then, on July 7, 1998, Rudolph approached George Nordmann. Rudolph had known Nordmann since Rudolph was a teenager. By 1998, Nordmann was in his seventies, but

MALICIOUSLY DAMAGED, BY MEANS OF AN EXPLOSIVE DEVICE, BUILDINGS AND PROPERTY AFFECTING INTERSTATE COMMERCE WHICH RESULTED IN DEATH AND INJURY

ERIC ROBERT RUDOLPH

Date of photograph unknown   Date of photograph unknown   Date of Sketch July 1998

Aliases   Bob Randolph, Robert Randolph, Bob Rudolph, Eric Rudolph and Eric R. Rudolph.

DESCRIPTION

Date of Birth:	September 19, 1966	**Hair:**	Brown
Place of Birth:	Merritt Island, Florida	**Eyes:**	Blue
Height:	5'11"	**Complexion:**	Fair
Weight:	165 to 180 pounds	**Sex:**	Male
Build:	Medium	**Race:**	White
Occupation(s):	Carpenter, roofer and handyman	**Nationality:**	American
Scars and Marks:	He has a noticeable scar on his chin.		
Remarks:	None		

The FBI posted an official notice about Rudolph on its Ten Most Wanted Fugitives website.

he was still living in the same area and running his health food store in Andrews, North Carolina. Rudolph offered Nordmann cash for supplies and the use of a car. Rudolph had lost a lot of weight since January, and he told Nordmann he was "starving."[12] He also had a long beard and long hair tied in a ponytail. Nordmann gave Rudolph a bag of food but said he needed time to pray about providing further assistance.

Rudolph returned two days later to see what Nordmann had decided. Nordmann was not home, but he had left bags of food and supplies in the kitchen along with a note. The note said that Rudolph could not use one of Nordmann's cars. Rudolph disregarded the note and stole one of Nordmann's old trucks. He packed the food and supplies into the truck and left Nordmann $500 in cash. The money was all in $100 bills.[13]

Two more days passed. It was July 11 before Nordmann reported Rudolph's visit to law enforcement. Some believed

Nordmann had been too shocked or afraid to report Rudolph to officials earlier. Others believed he sympathized with Rudolph's views. Whatever the reason, Rudolph's interaction with Nordmann would be the last documented sighting of Rudolph for almost five years. On July 13, law enforcement located the stolen truck at a forest campground more than 50 miles (80 km) away.[15] There was no sign of Rudolph.

BOMB ATTACKS

- July 27, 1996: Centennial Olympic Park, Atlanta, Georgia

- January 16, 1997: Northside Family Planning Services, Sandy Springs, Georgia

- February 21, 1997: Otherside Lounge, Atlanta, Georgia

- January 29, 1998: New Woman All Women Health Clinic, Birmingham, Alabama

A COLD TRAIL

The search for Rudolph intensified after Nordmann reported his encounter with him. Law enforcement homed in on the area where Nordmann's truck had been discovered. Agents divided into teams of six to eight to take different trails through the North Carolina forests.[1] As they entered the trails, they remained heavily armed, and search dogs were still on hand. Helicopters continued flying overhead. The search operated day and night. The media followed developments with intense coverage.

Agents found several campsites, and they connected at least one to Rudolph through fingerprints on trash buried there. They also found cans of food that matched items on a grocery store receipt they found in his truck. However, the teams thought these were old findings connected to Rudolph's movements before he confronted Nordmann. There were no fresh sightings of Rudolph by agents on the ground.

Police helicopters tried to spot Rudolph from above, but the dense forest made it difficult to see anything on the ground.

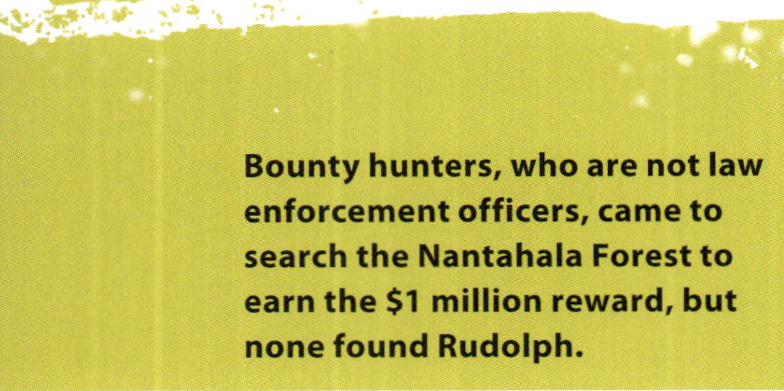

Helicopter searches also did not produce any sightings. In the summer months, the helicopters had limited visibility due to the forest cover. A spokesperson for the SBTF said, "With that triple canopy of high pines and hardwoods and incredibly thick brush, you couldn't see a [vehicle]. It's incredibly difficult."[2]

New Tactics

By October 1998, the SBTF had gathered enough evidence to bring legal charges against Rudolph for all three Atlanta attacks—the Olympic Park bombing, the Sandy Springs clinic bombing, and the Otherside Lounge bombing. FBI director Louis Freeh called specific attention to the Olympic Park bombing in a statement about the charges. Freeh said, "The fatal bombing in Atlanta was a terrorist attack aimed at thousands of innocent persons gathered at the Olympic Park. Within the FBI's Domestic Terrorism Program, there is no higher priority than the capture of Eric Robert Rudolph."[3] Officials had already filed charges against Rudolph for the Birmingham bombing in February.

Throughout the fall, law enforcement continued to expand its search tactics. Some agents received expert training on how to recognize and search old mines and caves. The area had hundreds of caves. Some of these were known and marked on maps. Others were hidden and uncharted. Some were so disguised by plant growth that a person could pass within feet of a cave entrance and never know it was there.

Law enforcement did not believe Rudolph would use these caves as long-term shelter. They could be unstable, and air did not circulate well through them. Without air circulation, it could become dangerous to breathe. However, agents thought he might use the caves as places to store supplies and take refuge for short periods.

With its caves, mines, and craggy landscape, western North Carolina provided Rudolph with virtually limitless places to hide.

The SBTF also boosted the number of agents on-site in western North Carolina. The number had fallen to about 80 after the intensified search in July produced no sightings.[4] In the fall, the SBTF again brought in more agents, because its leadership believed the cool weather might provide new search opportunities.

Agents thought helicopter searches could be more effective with the leaves gone from the trees in autumn. They also believed that heat-sensing technology would work better in the cold fall and winter weather. In the cold, heat from campfires or a live human body would be more noticeable compared with the rest of the environment. Despite law enforcement's hopes for better results in the fall and winter, they still did not find Rudolph.

Theories about the Fugitive's Location

Many theories emerged to account for the lack of progress in the case. There were some who thought Rudolph may have escaped to another part of the country or gone abroad. At various points in the search, reports came from Colorado, Mexico, Canada, and other places, but none produced credible leads. One of Rudolph's family members thought he may have gone to Germany because of his interest in Nazism or to the Netherlands because of his background in growing marijuana.

People who knew Rudolph reported that he had been to both countries earlier in his life.

Others thought he might be receiving help to remain hidden and alive in the western North Carolina area. They speculated that help might have been coming from quietly sympathetic local citizens or from militant extremists in the region. Letters sent after the Sandy Springs, Otherside Lounge, and Birmingham bombings referenced the Army of God. Investigators searched extensively for a link between Rudolph and members of that group or other militant organizations. They conducted hundreds of interviews. There was no indication that Rudolph had collaborated with other extremists during the bombings or while he was in hiding. Instead, the evidence indicated that Rudolph continued to act as a lone wolf.

Still others believed Rudolph was dead. Among those was John Magaw,

MYSTERIOUS BREAK-INS

During the manhunt, there were reports of intrusions in cabins and summer homes scattered throughout the mountains of western North Carolina. These places could be empty for weeks or months because they were used as vacation spots and not permanent homes. The intruder did not take valuable items or damage property. Instead, they would take everyday supplies such as soap, socks, food, and paper towels. Sometimes there was evidence that the intruder had taken a shower or shaved in the bathroom. Law enforcement suspected Rudolph in these break-ins.

the director of the ATF. In December 1999, Magaw said, "My gut instinct is that he is still there, in a cave, and he's dead. That's only my opinion."[5] Magaw was retiring as director at the time of his comment. Agents still active on the SBTF emphasized that they could not make assumptions without forensic evidence. The task force did not yet have any forensic evidence of Rudolph's death.

Should the Search Continue?

By the middle of 2001, three years into the manhunt, the expenses totaled approximately $20 million.[6] Nevertheless, the SBTF insisted that it would not quit. In March 2001, FBI spokesman Patrick Crosby said, "We're not going to give up. There are too many victims, too many people hurt. . . . Even if it was one victim, these are serious federal crimes that will be aggressively pursued."[7]

The SBTF also justified the manhunt as a deterrent to Rudolph even if he had not yet been captured. They argued that attention during the early phases of the manhunt and the ongoing effort in later years prevented him from committing other attacks. One agent said, "We wanted to catch him, but we also wanted to make sure he didn't strike again. I'm convinced that the investment . . . saved lives."[8] Rudolph remained on the FBI's Ten Most Wanted list.

Turning to Local Forces

Though the SBTF justified the continued search, it reduced the number of agents in western North Carolina. In the second half of 1999 and into 2000, there were just a dozen federal agents on the scene.[9] In March 2000, the SBTF released a statement that its command post in Andrews would close that June. Agents had been using the location as the center of their operations since the fall of 1998. It had been a strong presence in the area, with armed guards and barbed wire surrounding the premises as protection.

By 2003, five years into the search, just two agents remained.[10] They were based in Asheville, a city a little more than 100 miles (161 km) northeast of Murphy. These agents sent local scouts out on targeted searches when they received tips or leads. The scouts were paid for their work, but they were not law enforcement agents. Instead, they were outdoorspeople

SBTF TIMELINE

MARCH 1998

The Department of Justice creates the Southeast Bomb Task Force (SBTF).

JULY 1998

Law enforcement locates a truck Rudolph stole at a campground in North Carolina. Teams of agents begin searching the area. After an intensified search turns up no leads, the number of agents on the scene falls to about 80.

OCTOBER 1998

The SBTF brings legal charges against Rudolph for the three Atlanta-area attacks. The task force brings more agents into the manhunt in western North Carolina, hoping the conditions in fall and winter will make it easier to find him.

LATE 1999–EARLY 2000

The number of federal agents involved in the search for Rudolph in North Carolina falls to only a dozen.

MARCH 2000

The SBTF announces that its command post in Andrews, North Carolina, will close in June.

2003

Two federal agents remain on the case in Asheville, North Carolina.

who lived in the area and knew it well. Law enforcement recognized their expertise and saw it as a valuable source of help. They were used to hiking challenging trails, observing the conditions, and handling difficult weather.

Investigators also asked local hunters going about their regular activities to watch for new tracks or camps that might suggest Rudolph's presence. They said, "We still see local law enforcement and citizen help to be a key in finding Rudolph."[11] After all, local residents had been key to other breaks in the case. For example, it had been Birmingham citizens who recorded Rudolph's license plate number after the bombing in their city.

CHAPTER EIGHT

FINDING A FUGITIVE

Officer Jeff Postell of the Murphy Police Department was doing his patrol in the early morning hours of the overnight shift on May 31, 2003. At that time of day, he was the only one on patrol duty checking the streets for suspicious activity. There were just ten full-time officers because the town of Murphy was so small.[1]

In 2003, Postell was a rookie. He was 21 years old and had been on the police force in Murphy for just ten months. Postell's training taught him many things, including the importance of varying his patrol route. Driving the same route day after day could give criminals valuable information. They could observe law enforcement patterns and learn how to avoid the police. At about 3:30 a.m. on May 31, his new patrol route took him around a shopping center where he saw something unusual.

Murphy Police officer Jeff Postell played a crucial role in bringing the long saga of the Olympic Park bomber to a close.

There was a man searching a dumpster by the Save-A-Lot grocery store.

A Prowler in the Dark

It was a white man who appeared to be in his thirties. The man had short, dark hair and a mustache. He was thin but otherwise looked healthy. He wore a camouflage jacket and sneakers. He also had a backpack, and he was carrying an object Postell thought might be a weapon. When the man saw Postell, he fled and tried to hide behind a stack of discarded milk crates. The police officer drew his gun and ordered the man to come out. He did, and Postell apprehended him.

What Postell thought might have been a weapon turned out to be a flashlight. The man was not armed. He told Postell that he was a homeless hitchhiker from Ohio named Jerry Wilson, but he had no identification with him. He gave Postell a birth date, but when Postell checked the name and birth date in the police database, there was no match.

A suspicious man behind an ordinary Save-A-Lot grocery store on a spring day in 2003 ended up being the target of a years-long manhunt.

Though the man was not armed, Postell thought his story and behavior were suspicious. Officers who arrived as backup agreed. They believed he was lying about who he was. In fact, one of the backup officers, Sean Matthews, commented that the man looked like the wanted fugitive Eric Rudolph.

An Outlaw Uncovered

Postell initially took Matthews's comment as a joke. However, he agreed they needed more information about the man. With the handcuffed man secured in his patrol car, Postell drove to the local jail. On the ride, Postell said the man stared at

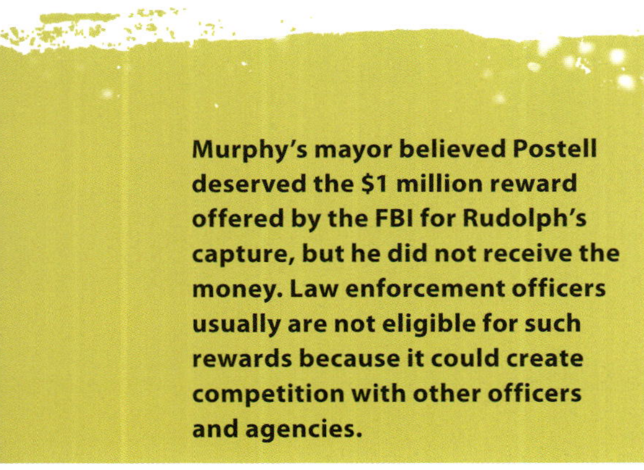

him and "had the coldest eyes."[2] It seemed that he was muttering something about being "glad it's over" and "tired of running."[3] Other than that, Postell remembers the arrest being uneventful, and the man complied with orders.

Still, Matthews's suggestion about the man's identity nagged at Postell as he drove on.

At the jail, the officers investigated Matthews's suspicions about the man. They looked at the FBI's current Ten Most Wanted Fugitives list and printed off the posting for Rudolph. The posting described a white man in his thirties with brown hair, blue eyes, a scar on his chin, and a height of about five feet, 11 inches (1.8 m). It described fine details like the shape of his ears and his hairline. The posting also listed Rudolph's crime: causing death and damage with an explosive device.

The man sitting in the Murphy jail fit the FBI's description. Postell's fellow officer had been right. The man searching the dumpster was Rudolph. When police made the connection, the man said, "I'm Eric Robert Rudolph, and you've got me."[4] Rudolph had escaped capture for more than five years. It was Postell on a routine patrol who finally caught him.

Conversations in the Local Jail

Rudolph's capture had taken place on a Saturday, and he remained in the local jail over the weekend. After that, Rudolph would be moved to Asheville to appear in federal court. The federal court would decide how the legal cases against Rudolph would proceed.

At the local jail, officers were surprised at Rudolph's appearance after five years in hiding. He was thinner than he had been when he disappeared. Otherwise, he seemed clean and healthy. He had some stubble on his chin, but his mustache was neat and his hair had been cut. He wore a jacket and sneakers. This appearance made officers question what had happened in his time as a fugitive. There was more suspicion about whether others had helped him with supplies or shelter.

The officers brought Rudolph a mattress and food, and he began to open up to them about his time as a fugitive. Rudolph told them he hunted animals for food,

OVERNIGHT CELEBRITY

In the days and weeks after Rudolph's arrest, Postell received a lot of attention. Fans sent him letters, and media outlets requested interviews. *People* magazine named him as one of its top 25 bachelors of the year. The attention even followed Postell as he continued his police work. He remembered, "I had people actually want me to write them tickets just to have my autograph."[5]

including turkeys, bears, wild boar, and deer. He also gathered acorns, berries, and other sources of plant food. Sometimes he ate salamanders. He mentioned stealing food from populated areas, but he did not mention receiving help from individuals.

Rudolph also told local police that he moved constantly in the Nantahala Forest for the first few months. Later he established a base camp in the mountains and another camp closer to Murphy. He showed officers the camp locations on a map.

Searching the Camps

The mountain camp was at Fires Creek, about 12 miles (19 km) from Murphy.[6] The location offered protection in multiple ways. It was on top of a steep ridge that was difficult to climb on foot. It was shielded by evergreen trees that made it hard to spot from helicopters overhead. Hunters were not allowed in this particular area because it was in a wildlife management zone.

At the camp, investigators found clothing, cooking supplies, reading material, a radio, toiletries, a sleeping bag, and even a news article about being named to the FBI's Ten Most Wanted list. There was a spring for fresh water and a firepit for cooking. Agents found animal bones and other remains. There were also large barrels for food and supplies. They were stocked with soy, oats, and other grains and dried foods. Some of these were hung in the trees to keep bears away while others were buried in the ground. Rudolph kept a rifle and ammunition at the camp.

The second camp was close to a populated area. It overlooked Murphy. From it, Rudolph could see the town's high school, a grocery store, and a restaurant. This camp also had toiletries, reading material, and a spring for water. There were barrels here too, and investigators also found a makeshift cooler placed in the spring. Rudolph used the cooler to store food he took from dumpsters. When investigators arrived to search it, they discovered tacos inside.

Over time, agents learned that Rudolph had used other small camps, caves, and hiding places for supplies and to

FBI agents closely examined the campsites where Rudolph had been hiding out.

monitor search activity. They continued to believe that Rudolph

broke into cabins left empty during the winter to survive

the cold. There were many who continued to think Rudolph

had received help to stay hidden and alive, including some in

the law enforcement community. Rudolph maintained that he had no help, and law enforcement did not find evidence of help aside from the 1998 encounter that George Nordmann had reported to police.

SENTENCED TO LIFE

On April 8, 2005, the Department of Justice announced that Rudolph had taken a plea agreement. According to the agreement, Rudolph would plead guilty to the bombings at Centennial Olympic Park, the Sandy Springs clinic, the Otherside Lounge, and the Birmingham clinic. In exchange, the death penalty was removed as a sentencing option. Rudolph received four life sentences without the possibility of parole.[1] Officials placed Rudolph in a maximum security prison, known as a supermax facility, in Colorado to serve the sentences.

New Information Revealed

Rudolph's lawyers released a statement from him after his guilty plea. It was a written statement of 11 pages and contained long passages on his political views. It also contained

Rudolph was kept under heavy guard after being taken into custody.

FBI
ATF

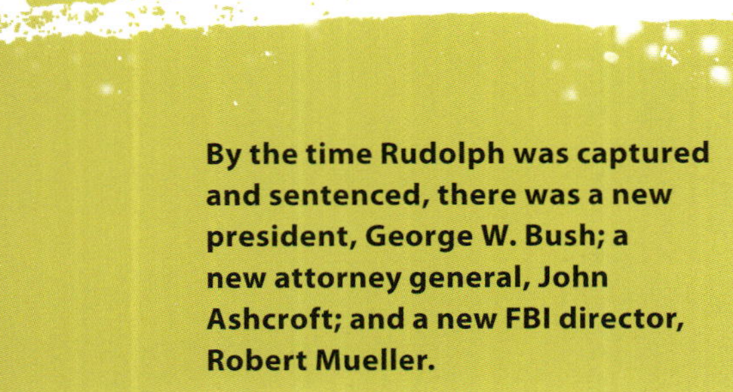

details about the bombings and his time in hiding. For example, Rudolph recounted that the Olympic Park bombing had not gone as planned. He intended to set off five bombs over five days. There would have been a 911 phone call warning of the bombs 40 to 45 minutes before each explosion. The calls were meant to draw law enforcement to the area as targets.

Rudolph placed the first bomb in Centennial Olympic Park and then left to make the 911 phone call. The call before the first bombing had not gone as planned. The 911 operator disconnected Rudolph's call before he could deliver his full message. To avoid being traced, he went to another phone booth and placed a second call. At that phone booth, Rudolph feared witnesses could overhear him. He cut the call short. After that, Rudolph abandoned the plan for the other four Olympic bombings.

Passages about his time in hiding explained how he avoided detection. For instance, he wrote that he hid from helicopters in a small dugout covered by a rock. This prevented the heat-sensing equipment on the helicopters from detecting his body.

These passages also revealed that he was close to civilization during parts of that time. For example, he observed law enforcement activity. He monitored the agents at their Andrews command post and then at their smaller Murphy office. He got an idea to bomb the Andrews post in the summer of 1999. However, he could not arrange the attack because he had to spend so much time collecting food. He decided to try the plan again in the fall of 2000 when the agents had moved to the Murphy office. He constructed a device, monitored the agents' movements, and positioned the bomb. However, Rudolph stopped the plan at the last minute. He also planned an abortion clinic bombing in Asheville just before the 2000 election. He had to abandon that plan when the truck he stole broke down.

Rudolph revealed more about his time in hiding in an autobiography he self-published in 2013 with the help of his brother Daniel. On his own in the mountains, Rudolph nearly starved. He needed resources from society. The autobiography described how Rudolph watched Nordmann's daily routine and trespassed on his property many times in secret before approaching him. He took fresh eggs from the chickens in Nordmann's yard, picked fruit from his trees, stocked up on supplies from the basement, and cooked and bathed inside the house. He watched movies from Nordmann's collection.

Rudolph then developed the habit of searching dumpsters behind stores and fast-food restaurants. He would also steal from grain silos and people's gardens and homes. There were many near misses with other people. Rudolph even claimed that two police officers who did not recognize him stopped to help him when a truck he had stolen ran out of gas.

Jeff Postell, the officer who had captured Rudolph, characterized the autobiography as a way for him to seek attention. Postell also believed it could be a source of pain for survivors. Government officials said that Rudolph could not keep any money the autobiography might earn. Part of Rudolph's plea deal was more than $1 million in restitution to the victims.[5]

Capturing National Attention

There are various ideas about why the case gained so much public attention. Some of these ideas focus on where and when it occurred. Rudolph's first bombing at Centennial Olympic Park struck a major international venue with athletes, spectators, and reporters from around the world. People closely followed

John Hawthorne, *right*, the husband of Olympic Park bombing victim Alice Hawthorne, spoke to the press after Rudolph's sentencing. Standing nearby was their daughter Fallon, *center*, who had survived the attack.

An FBI agent gave members of the news media tours of Rudolph's hiding spots. In the age of 24-hour news, an enormous amount of media attention focused on the case.

the news of the attack and the investigation afterward. There were millions of eyes on the events as they unfolded.

The bombings and manhunt also occurred soon after other domestic terrorism incidents that had attracted national attention. These included Timothy McVeigh's attack in Oklahoma City in 1995 and Unabomber Ted Kaczynski's capture in April 1996. People followed the Olympic Park bombing, Rudolph's other bombings, and the manhunt wondering if these kinds of domestic attacks were emerging as a threatening trend.

Other theories about the attention given to the Olympic Park bombing focused on the media.

The media played a strong role in promoting the story from the beginning. The Olympic Park bombing occurred at a time when the 24-hour cable news cycle was just beginning. The 24-hour news cycle meant nonstop coverage. Henry Schuster was a producer at CNN when the bombing occurred. In a 2019 article, he wrote that constant news coverage could bring "a rush to judgement."[6] This problem became evident in Richard Jewell's treatment. The media immediately cast Jewell under harsh scrutiny before a methodical investigation had progressed.

Media attention also remained intense early in the manhunt and then again when Rudolph was captured. The media captured dramatic images of armed agents and high-tech search equipment. One local resident commented that the heavy law enforcement approach also attracted attention to the case. He said, "[People] think he's one man and they've got all these people and all this sophisticated equipment looking for him. It sort of makes him an underdog."[7]

Another resident said that it was "human nature" to be drawn to underdog stories.[9]

There were also other elements of the story that interested people. One was the concept of a single person against nature. Rudolph faced a rough natural environment in the Appalachian Mountains. Potentially deadly obstacles included exposure to bad weather, predatory animals, steep climbs and sharp drop-offs, starvation, injury, and illness. Like underdog stories, stories of human survival naturally draw people in.

The Appalachian Mountains of North Carolina also had a reputation as being an isolated, mysterious place where militant and outlaw culture thrived. Jerry Clark, a retired FBI special agent, and Ed Palattella, a crime journalist, believe fugitives and manhunts attract attention because they are exciting. "Most everyone likes a good chase," they wrote in the book *On the Lam: A History of Hunting Fugitives in America*.[10] Forensic psychologist Richard Lettieri has written about the interest in crime stories more generally. Lettieri argues the interest is about looking at the bad parts of human behavior. In an article for *Psychology Today*, Lettieri wrote that crime stories are a way of "facing that dark side."[11] The attack at Olympic Park and the subsequent hunt for the bomber was one of the most famous examples of this in the history of American crime.

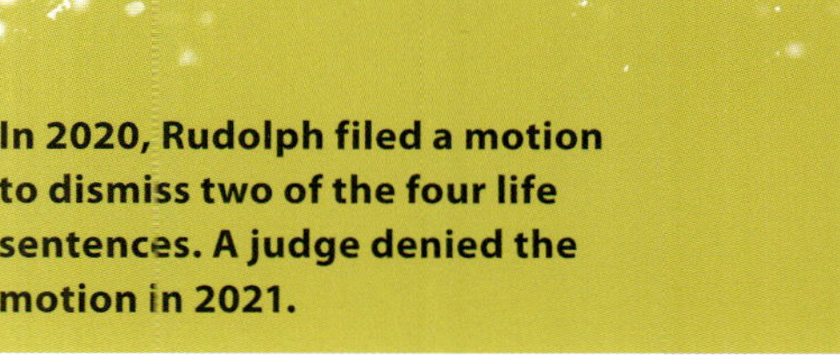

TIMELINE

1996

- On June 27, a bomb explodes in Centennial Olympic Park in Atlanta, Georgia, causing two deaths and injuring more than 100 people.

- On July 30, the *Atlanta Journal-Constitution* publishes an article reporting that the FBI suspects security guard Richard Jewell as the bomber.

- On October 26, the authorities release a statement saying that Jewell is no longer a target of the investigation.

- On December 9, the FBI releases the audio recording of 911 phone calls placed by the Olympic Park bomber in hopes of bringing in new leads.

1997

- On January 16, two bombs explode and cause several injuries at Sandy Springs Professional Building just north of Atlanta.

- On February 21, one bomb explodes and causes several injuries at the Otherside Lounge in Atlanta. A second unexploded device is found by responders.

1998

- On January 29, a bomb explodes at the New Woman All Women Health Clinic in Birmingham, Alabama, killing a security guard. Later that day, two witnesses report the license plate number of a suspicious person seen near the Birmingham clinic bombing.

- On January 30, Eric Rudolph flees into North Carolina's Nantahala National Forest and a manhunt begins.

- In February, authorities file charges against Rudolph in the Birmingham bombing.

- In March, the Department of Justice creates the Southeast Bomb Task Force (SBTF) to coordinate investigations in North Carolina, Georgia, and Alabama.

- On May 5, the FBI adds Rudolph to its Ten Most Wanted Fugitives list and offers a $1 million reward for information that would help locate Rudolph.

- On July 7, Rudolph approaches George Nordmann in Andrews, North Carolina, to ask for supplies.

- In October, officials file charges against Rudolph for the three Atlanta-area bombings.

2000

- In June, the SBTF closes its command center in Andrews but continues to pursue new leads in the hunt for Rudolph.

2003

- On May 31, police officer Jeff Postell captures Eric Rudolph behind a grocery store in Murphy, North Carolina.

2005

- On April 8, the Department of Justice announces that Rudolph has taken a plea agreement for life in prison without parole.

ESSENTIAL FACTS

SIGNIFICANT EVENTS

- Around 1:20 a.m. on July 27, 1996, a bomb explodes at Centennial Olympic Park in Atlanta, Georgia. One person is killed by shrapnel from the bomb, and another dies of a heart attack rushing to get to the bomb site.

- In January and February of 1997, there are two more bombings in the Atlanta area. The first occurs at an abortion clinic on January 16, and the second occurs at a gay and lesbian bar on February 21.

- On January 29, 1998, a bomb explodes at an abortion clinic in Birmingham, Alabama. Two witnesses record Eric Rudolph's license plate number as he leaves the scene.

- On May 31, 2003, police officer Jeff Postell captures Rudolph in Murphy, North Carolina, ending a five-year manhunt.

- On April 8, 2005, the Department of Justice announces that Rudolph has taken a plea agreement. Rudolph receives four life sentences.

KEY PLAYERS

- Eric Rudolph was a serial bomber responsible for four bombings in Georgia and Alabama between July 1996 and January 1998.

- Richard Jewell was a security guard falsely accused of setting off the bomb in Centennial Olympic Park.

- Louis Freeh was the FBI director during Rudolph's bombings and the first three years of the manhunt for him.

- Jermaine Hughes was the first witness who followed Rudolph and reported his license plate number to law enforcement after the 1998 bombing in Birmingham, Alabama.

- Jeff Postell was the rookie police officer who arrested Rudolph in 2003.

IMPACT ON SOCIETY

The 1996 bombing in Centennial Olympic Park came at a time when concerns about domestic terrorism were growing. The search for Olympic Park bomber Eric Rudolph was one of the longest and most expensive manhunts the country had ever seen. It showed the impact media can have on investigations and on private citizens. It also revealed problems and tensions in law enforcement investigative work. At the same time, it encouraged law enforcement to consider how local, state, and federal agencies could work together effectively. It shed light on extremism and militant movements within the United States.

Rudolph's bombings made clear the damaging toll of terrorism on civilians. They also demonstrated the pivotal role individual citizens and local communities can have in countering extremist violence. True crime films, podcasts, and books continue to examine the bombings and the subsequent manhunt.

QUOTE

"The fatal bombing in Atlanta was a terrorist attack aimed at thousands of innocent persons gathered at the Olympic Park. Within the FBI's Domestic Terrorism Program, there is no higher priority than the capture of Eric Robert Rudolph."

—*Louis Freeh, FBI director, October 1998*

GLOSSARY

accomplice
Someone who helps someone else carry out a task. Often used to describe someone who has helped commit a crime.

anti-government
Opposed to the government, especially the national government.

apocalyptic
Relating to a destructive end of the world.

discharge
To release from the military.

extremist
Having ideas that most others find to be radical or unreasonable; a person who holds such ideas.

federal government
The government at the national level.

forensic
Characterized by the use of scientific techniques to investigate a crime.

fugitive
A criminal who flees or hides to escape law enforcement.

GED

The credential received by passing the General Education Development Tests, a group of academic tests that people can take to earn a certification equivalent to a high school diploma.

lead

Information that moves an investigation forward.

person of interest

A person being watched or questioned in connection with a crime but who is not yet an accused suspect.

plea deal

An agreement between prosecutors and a defendant in which the defendant will plead guilty in exchange for reduced charges or a lesser sentence.

projectile

An object launched through the air.

shrapnel

Debris released by an explosion.

suspect

A person thought to have committed a crime.

warrant

A court document allowing law enforcement to carry out an arrest or a search.

ADDITIONAL RESOURCES

SELECTED BIBLIOGRAPHY

Alexander, Kent, and Kevin Salwen. *The Suspect: An Olympic Bombing, the FBI, the Media, and Richard Jewell, the Man Caught in the Middle*. Abrams, 2020.

Freeman, Scott. "Fallout: An Oral History of the Olympic Park Bombing." *Atlanta Magazine*, 1 July 2011, atlantamagazine.com. Accessed 2 June 2023.

Vollers, Maryanne. *Lone Wolf: Eric Rudolph: Murder, Myth, and the Pursuit of an American Outlaw*. Harper Perennial, 2007.

FURTHER READINGS

Marcovitz, Hal. *Domestic Extremism: How Big Is the Threat?* ReferencePoint, 2022.

Murray, Laura K. *Domestic Terrorism*. Abdo, 2021.

Streissguth, Tom. *The Unabomber*. Abdo, 2024.

ONLINE RESOURCES

To learn more about the Olympic Park bombing, please visit **abdobooklinks.com** or scan this QR code. These links are routinely monitored and updated to provide the most current information available.

MORE INFORMATION

For more information on this subject, contact or visit the following organizations:

ATLANTA HISTORY CENTER

130 W. Paces Ferry Rd. NW

Atlanta, GA 30305

atlantahistorycenter.com/buildings-and-grounds/atlanta-history-museum/

This history center includes an exhibit about the 1996 Olympic Games that explores how the major event shaped the city of Atlanta.

ATLANTA JOURNAL-CONSTITUTION

6205 Peachtree Dunwoody Rd.

Sandy Springs, GA 30328

ajc.com

The *Atlanta Journal-Constitution*, a newspaper in Atlanta, covered the 1996 Olympic Games and Eric Rudolph's bombings. It published the first article about the FBI's investigation of Richard Jewell.

TERRORISM RESEARCH CENTER

211 Old Main

University of Arkansas

Fayetteville, AR 72701

terrorismresearch.uark.edu

The Terrorism Research Center is a federally funded organization run through the Department of Sociology and Criminology at the University of Arkansas. The center collaborates with many other organizations and provides programs for students on how to track and analyze crimes.

SOURCE NOTES

CHAPTER 1. AN EXPLOSION IN THE NIGHT

1. Kent Alexander and Kevin Salwen. *The Suspect: An Olympic Bombing, the FBI, the Media, and Richard Jewell, the Man Caught in the Middle*. Abrams, 2020. 3.

2. Alexander and Salwen, *The Suspect*, 1.

3. Scott Freeman. "Fallout." *Atlanta*, 1 July 2011, atlantamagazine.com. Accessed 14 July 2023.

4. Freeman, "Fallout."

5. "Olympic Park Bombing Fast Facts." *CNN*, 6 July 2023, cnn.com. Accessed 14 July 2023.

6. Shaila Dewan. "Olympics Bomber Apologizes and Is Sentenced to Life Terms." *New York Times*, 23 Aug. 2005, nytimes.com. Accessed 14 July 2023.

7. Freeman, "Fallout."

8. Freeman, "Fallout."

9. Freeman, "Fallout."

10. William Drozdiak. "FBI Probes Bombing as Olympic Games Continue." *Washington Post*, 28 July 1996, washingtonpost.com. Accessed 14 July 2023.

11. Alexander and Salwen, *The Suspect*, 87.

12. "The Oklahoma City Bombing 20 Years Later." *Federal Bureau of Investigation*, n.d., stories.fbi.gov. Accessed 14 July 2023.

13. "The Unabomber." *FBI*, n.d., fbi.gov. Accessed 14 July 2023.

14. "The President's Radio Address and an Exchange with Reporters, July 27, 1996." *GovInfo*, n.d., govinfo.gov. Accessed 14 July 2023.

15. James Doubek. "50 Years Ago, the Munich Olympics Massacre Changed How We Think about Terrorism." *NPR*, 4 Sept. 2022, npr.org. Accessed 14 July 2023.

CHAPTER 2. THE ACCUSATION

1. Kent Alexander and Kevin Salwen. *The Suspect: An Olympic Bombing, the FBI, the Media, and Richard Jewell, the Man Caught in the Middle*. Abrams, 2020. 95.

2. Alexander and Salwen, *The Suspect*, 122.

3. Alexander and Salwen, *The Suspect*, 127.

4. Alexander and Salwen, *The Suspect*, 126.

5. Scott Freeman. "Presumed Guilty." *Atlanta*, 1 Dec. 1996, atlantamagazine.com. Accessed 14 July 2023.

6. "'I Am Not the Olympic Park Bomber.'" *CNN*, 28 Oct. 1996, cnn.com. Accessed 14 July 2023.

7. "Statement on Jewell." *New York Times*, 27 Oct. 1996, nytimes.com. Accessed 14 July 2023.

8. Alexander and Salwen, *The Suspect*, 173.

9. Alexander and Salwen, *The Suspect*, 289.

10. "Governor Perdue Commends Richard Jewell." *Governor Sonny Perdue*, 1 Aug. 2006, sonnyperdue.georgia.gov. Accessed 14 July 2023.

CHAPTER 3. TWO MORE ATTACKS IN ATLANTA

1. Kevin Sack. "FBI Reward of $500,000 in Olympic Bombing Case." *New York Times*, 10 Dec. 1996, nytimes.com. Accessed 14 July 2023.

2. Kevin Sack. "In Latest Atlanta Bombing, 5 Are Injured at a Gay Bar." *New York Times*, 23 Feb. 1997, nytimes.com. Accessed 14 July 2023.

3. Sack, "5 Are Injured at a Gay Bar."

4. John Burnett. "Two Decades Later, Some Branch Davidians Still Believe." *NPR*, 20 Apr. 2013, npr.org. Accessed 14 July 2023.

5. "'Army of God' Informs FBI It Bombed Clinic, Nightclub." *Roanoke Times*, 25 Feb. 1997, scholar.lib.vt.edu. Accessed 14 July 2023.

6. "'Army of God' Informs FBI."

CHAPTER 4. THE PURSUIT BEGINS

1. Maryanne Vollers. *Lone Wolf: Eric Rudolph and the Legacy of American Terror*. Harper Perennial, 2007. 48.

2. Kent Alexander and Kevin Salwen. *The Suspect: An Olympic Bombing, the FBI, the Media, and Richard Jewell, the Man Caught in the Middle*. Abrams, 2020. 292.

3. Alexander and Salwen, *The Suspect*, 292.

4. John Christensen. "Where's Eric Rudolph?" *CNN*, 5 Mar. 2001, edition.cnn.com. Accessed 14 July 2023.

5. Alexander and Salwen, *The Suspect*, 293.

CHAPTER 5. A LONE TERRORIST

1. Maryanne Vollers. *Lone Wolf: Eric Rudolph and the Legacy of American Terror*. Harper Perennial, 2007. 95.

2. "Deborah Rudolph Speaks Out about Her Former Brother- n-Law, Olympic Park Bomber Eric Robert Rudolph." *Southern Poverty Law Center*, 29 Nov. 2001, splcenter.org. Accessed 14 July 2023.

3. Vollers, *Lone Wolf*, 104.

4. Kate Zernike. "A Life Marked by Loyalty, Self-Sufficiency and Deep Hatred." *New York Times*, 2 June 2003, nytimes.com. Accessed 14 July 2023.

5. Kent Alexander and Kevin Salwen. *The Suspect: An Olympic Bombing, the FBI, the Media, and Richard Jewell, the Man Caught in the Middle*. Abrams, 2020. 220.

CHAPTER 6. LAUNCHING A MANHUNT

1. Kent Alexander and Kevin Salwen. *The Suspect: An Olympic Bombing, the FBI, the Media, and Richard Jewell, the Man Caught in the Middle*. Abrams, 2020. 294.

2. "Nantahala National Forest." *USDA*, n.d., fs.usda.gov. Accessed 14 July 2023.

3. Maryanne Vollers. *Lone Wolf: Eric Rudolph and the Legacy of American Terror*. Harper Perennial, 2007. 84–85.

4. "Art Harris: The Hunt for Eric Rudolph." *CNN*, 27 July 2001, cnn.com. Accessed 14 July 2023.

5. Kim Dinan. "The Hunt for Eric Rudolph." *Blue Ridge Outdoors*, 20 May 2018, blueridgeoutdoors.com. Accessed 14 July 2023.

6. Cynthia Lewis. "Whatever Happened to the Search for Eric Rudolph?" *Southern Cultures*, 2001, go.gale.com. Accessed 14 July 2023.

7. Dinan, "The Hunt for Eric Rudolph."

8. Lewis, "Whatever Happened to the Search for Eric Rudolph?"

9. "Justice Department, FBI, and ATF Announce Task Force to Investigate Series of Bombings in Southeast." *Department of Justice*, 17 Mar. 1998, justice.gov. Accessed 14 July 2023.

10. "Eric Rudolph." *FBI*, n.d., fbi.gov. Accessed 14 July 2023.

11. Edward Walsh. "FBI Increases Reward for Bombing Suspect." *Washington Post*, 6 May 1998, washingtonpost.com. Accessed 14 July 2023.

12. Alexander and Salwen, *The Suspect*, 301–302.

13. Alexander and Salwen, *The Suspect*, 303.

14. "Ten Most Wanted Fugitives FAQ." *FBI*, n.d., fbi.gov. Accessed 14 July 2023.

15. Alexander and Salwen, *The Suspect*, 303.

CHAPTER 7. A COLD TRAIL

1. Kevin Sack. "Elusive Bombing Fugitive Divides a Town." *New York Times*, 24 July 1998, nytimes.com. Accessed 14 July 2023.

2. John Christensen. "Where's Eric Rudolph?" *CNN*, 5 Mar. 2001, edition.cnn.com. Accessed 14 July 2023.

3. "Eric Rudolph Charged in Centennial Olympic Park Bombing." *Justice Department*, 14 Oct. 1998, justice.gov. Accessed 14 July 2023.

4. "Bullet Grazes FBI Agent Aiding Hunt for Serial Bomber." *Washington Post*, 13 Nov. 1998, washingtonpost.com. Accessed 14 July 2023.

5. "Officials, Victims Wonder about Eric Rudolph." *Greensboro News and Record*, 28 Jan. 2000, greensboro.com. Accessed 14 July 2023.

6. "Art Harris: The Hunt for Eric Rudolph." *CNN*, 27 July 2001, cnn.com. Accessed 14 July 2023.

7. Christensen, "Where's Eric Rudolph?"

8. "Eric Rudolph." *FBI*, n.d., fbi.gov. Accessed 14 July 2023.

9. Paul Nowell. "Search for Bombing Suspect Resumes." *Washington Post*, 12 July 1999, washingtonpost.com. Accessed 14 July 2023.

10. Jeffrey Gettleman. "Bomb Suspect's Picture of His Life in the Woods Draws Some Skepticism." *New York Times*, 8 June 2003, nytimes.com. Accessed 14 July 2023.

11. "Hunters Warned to Watch for Fugitive." *WFMY News 2*, 11 Nov. 2002, wfmynews2.com. Accessed 14 July 2023.

CHAPTER 8. FINDING A FUGITIVE

1. Michael Banks. "Man with Gaston County Ties Tells of How He Handcuffed Eric Rudolph." *Gaston Gazette*, 12 Dec. 2019, gastongazette.com. Accessed 14 July 2023.

2. Jeremy Markovich. "Here's What Happened to the Rookie NC Officer Who Nabbed Bomber Eric Rudolph." *WFAE 90.7*, 3 Dec. 2019, wfae.org. Accessed 14 July 2023.

3. Kim Dinan. "The Hunt for Eric Rudolph." *Blue Ridge Outdoors*, 20 May 2018, blueridgeoutdoors.com. Accessed 14 July 2023.

4. Markovich, "NC Officer Nabbed Rudolph."

5. Markovich, "NC Officer Nabbed Rudolph."

6. Maryanne Vollers. *Lone Wolf: Eric Rudolph and the Legacy of American Terror*. Harper Perennial, 2007. 196.

7. Vollers, *Lone Wolf*, 200.

CHAPTER 9. SENTENCED TO LIFE

1. "Eric Rudolph." *Bureau of Alcohol, Tobacco, Firearms and Explosives*, n.d., atf.gov. Accessed 14 July 2023.

2. "Rudolph Agrees to Plea Agreement." *CNN*, 12 Apr. 2005, cnn.com. Accessed 14 July 2023.

3. Cynthia Lewis. "Whatever Happened to the Search for Eric Rudolph?" *Southern Cultures*, 2001, go.gale.com. Accessed 14 July 2023.

4. "Eric Robert Rudolph to Plead Guilty to Serial Bombing Attacks in Atlanta and Birmingham." *Department of Justice*, 8 Apr. 2005, justice.gov. Accessed 14 July 2023.

5. "Eric Robert Rudolph Sentenced to Life in Prison for Birmingham Bombing Attack." *Department of Justice*, 18 July 2005, justice.gov. Accessed 14 July 2023.

6. Henry Schuster. "I Helped Make Richard Jewell Famous—and Ruined His Life in the Process." *Washington Post*, 6 Dec. 2019, washingtonpost.com. Accessed 14 July 2023.

7. Kevin Sack. "Elusive Bombing Fugitive Divides a Town." *New York Times*, 24 July 1998, nytimes.com. Accessed 14 July 2023.

8. Sack, "Elusive Bombing Fugitive."

9. Sack, "Elusive Bombing Fugitive."

10. Jerry Clark and Ed Palattella. *On the Lam: A History of Hunting Fugitives in America*. Rowman & Littlefield, 2019. 4.

11. Richard Lettieri. "Why Are We So Interested in Crime Stories?" *Psychology Today*, 24 Sept. 2021, psychologytoday.com. Accessed 14 July 2023.

INDEX

ABOUT THE AUTHOR

REBECCA MORRIS

Rebecca Morris is the author of several nonfiction books for students. She has degrees in English, international relations, and comparative humanities.